ANALYSIS OF CRICKET SKILLS

ANALYSIS OF CRICKET SKILLS

Dr. Vijay Kumar Srivastava
Reader,
Lakshmibai National Institute of Physical Education (LNIPE)
(Deemed University)
Mela Road, Gwalior (M.P.), INDIA

SPORTS PUBLICATION
G-6, 23/23-B, EMCA House, Ansari Road,
Darya Ganj, New Delhi-110 002
Ph.: (Off.) 65749511 (M) 9868028838
(Resi.) 27562163 E-mail: lakshaythani@hotmail.com

Published by:

SPORTS PUBLICATION
G-6, 23/23-B, EMCA House, Ansari Road,
Darya Ganj, New Delhi-110002
Phones : (O) 65749511 (R) 27562163, (M) 9868028838
E-mail: *ektathani@hotmail.com/ lakshaythani@hotmail.com*
Website: sportspublication.trade-india.com

I.S.B.N. – 81-7879-392-X

PRINTED IN INDIA 2007

Laser Typeset by:
JAIN MEDIA GRAPHICS,
C-4/95-A, Keshav Puram, Delhi-35. Ph.: 9911151534, 9350556511

Printed by:
CHAWLA OFFSET PRINTERS, Delhi-110052

Price: Rs. 200/-

CONTENTS

1

MECHANICAL ANALYSIS OF SELECTED BATTING

INTRODUCTION

Batting in cricket is a wonderful art, almost universal in appeal. People from very different parts of the world are often united in their appreciation of the flowing and rhythmical drives of a skilled batsman. Whether it is the majestic elegance of Sachin Tendulkar, the awesome power of Inzamam UL-Haq, or the brilliance of Aravinda de Silva, there is a certain poetry that captivates an audience And, great batsmanship is certainly not restricted to the present times! The past contains many more examples; the genius of Sir Donald Bradman, the brilliance of Sir Garfield Sobers, the technical perfection of Sunil Gavaskar, and the mystical artistry of K.S. Ranjitsinhji.

A question that naturally arises is: "Are great batsmen born or made?" Many are of the opinion that apart from teaching a few technical fundamentals, one's batting ability is determined early on in life that it is therefore counterproductive to scientifically investigate the principles of batting technique as this would just overcomplicate the act of striking a ball. In this article we have completed a qualitative biomechanical analysis of many aspects of batting technique. Our approach has generated a new set of batting principles, which can be supported by the methods of great batsmen. We will show that many of the established techniques of batting cannot be supported mechanically, and are not used by the elite players. Out objective is to present a solid technical framework that comes close to optimising the art of batting by making the act of striking a ball as simple as possible. Certainly, it is impossible to make every batsman a great one. However, through the wise use of qualitative biomechanical analysis, we believe that batting performance can be significantly improved, and that many good batsmen can be made into great ones.

What is it that makes a great batsman so different from a good one, or for that matter a poor one. Why did Sunil Gavaskar, that little master from India, have so much time to play the fastest bowlers in the world, when lesser batsmen were primarily concerned with their physical safety? How did the greatest of them all, sir Donald Bradman, achieve the unimaginable average of 99.94 runs per wicket? How did Sir Garfield sobers manage to totally dominate every bowling attack in the world with the most splendid array of shots, all executed with an ethereal elegance? And, what does the modern master, Sachin Tendulkar, possess, that makes him so much better than all the rest? Certainly, natural ability plays its part. However, we have found that the greatest batters share a common technical framework that makes it possible for them to optimise their ability

For those less well acquainted with the game of cricket, the technique of bating must seem exceedingly simple: just use a wooden bat to hit a ball that has been bowled from a distance of 22 yards, generally after it has bounced once off the ground. If so simple, how can certain batters hold the attention of millions of people for 3,4 or 5 days at a stretch? And why are elite batters prepared to spend countless hours perfecting their art in the practice nets, when they may be dismissed first ball in a game and have to wait days or sometimes weeks before they bat again? Conversely, what makes a batter bat for days on end when conditions may be excruciatingly difficult, and victory out of the question?

Those who know the game intimately are aware of the reasons for such rigorous practice. Batting is an art of infinite subtlety, not only in strategy, but also in its most basic mechanics. To be even moderately successful, a batter must have proficiency in a wide array of skills. On top of that, a batter has to know how to combat the almost unlimited variations concocted by the bowler=from variations in pace, length (the distance travelled before bouncing), and line of delivery, to swinging and swerving: motions dependent on the intricate combination of the seam angle and spin of the ball as it travels through the air. A further degree of complexity is introduced when the seam angle and spin are also used to change the line of the ball off the pitch.

The art of batting is batting is complex, and good batters are forever trying to master their craft. And for good reason - batting is probably the most complex sport to analyse mechanically. There are so many levers involved - all of them acting interdependently in response to the trajectory of the ball, and subject to a changeable number of constraints. The dynamics to describe such a situation would require a detailed mathematical model. This is one of the reasons that previous attempts to use biomechanics to evaluate batting technique have been simplistic, and of very little use to the coach. It is the view of the authors that the accepted biomechanical principles of batting have been developed without considering the appropriate constraints. As such, the implementation of these principles is unlikely to improve batting performance.

Even past elite players find it difficult to prescribe correct batting technique. Though they knew haw to bat proficiently, the execution of their skills was largely performed unconsciously. Therefore, it is often the case that an elite batsman's perception of what he is doing differs from what he is actually does. Unfortunately, this is when serious errors can be made in coaching.

In this article, we will discuss certain fundamental aspects of batting technique that are critical for elite performance. We will show that batting is a complex art, but that by using a qualitative biomechanical approach within the conceptual framework of optimization, it is possible to develop a set of technical principles that would make the art of batting more efficient. We believe that this is the first time batting has been analysed from a scientific viewpoint, and the results of our study can substantiated by the experiences and methods of the world's greatest batters. It also demonstrates the value of qualitative biomechanics, particularly when a quantitative approach is not possible either to the lack of proper testing equipment and facilities, or to experimental limits determined by the state of technology. At other times, a quantitative approach may not even be useful. All this demonstrates the need for biomechanics to develop strong skills in the art of qualitative analysis.; It is not an exact science, and the findings will evolve over time. But it is an indispensable tool to understand the biomechanical principles of complex human movement sequences. Batting falls under this category and as a first step requires the development of a qualitative biomechanical model. Only then can we begin to unravel the hidden secrets of the master batters of the past and present!

Developing a Qualitative Optimization Model

We developed a qualitative analysis model of batting bases on the rules of a standard optimization approach. Once the required output has been determined, then optimization problems, in general, are defined by three quantities: cost function, design variables, and constraint functions (*Nigg & Herzog.* (1955). The aim of the optimization is to minimize the cost function. We used this methodological approach to logically derive and present the qualitative mechanical principles that underlie elite batting technique. The skill therefore, lies in choosing the appropriate cost, design and constraint functions. This depends on the researcher's experience and mode of investigation. We based our choice of design constraints and variables from the exhaustive studies of elite players throughout the ages, and a consideration of rigid body dynamics principles.

An Introduction to the Initial Movement

In any analysis of batting technique, there is no better place to start than right at the beginning-just before the ball is released. The theoretical view that the batter remains perfectly balanced and completely uncommitted until ball release is virtually impossible to execute in practice. In fact there is no reason to suggest that there is an advantage in attempting this. It seems that a preliminary (or initial) movement before the ball is bowled is bowled is a natural reflexive response that causes the batter to adopt a quasi-static configuration with a specific set of dynamically induced muscle tensions throughout the body. From this initial position, the batter can then make a final decisive movement, either forward or back dependent on the trajectory and speed of the ball. This may seem an unnecessarily complex description for such a small movement. However, it should soon become apparent why this is necessary when we make the first attempts to optimise the preliminary movement.

Further evidence of the importance of the preliminary movement is substantiated by the experiences of past elite cricketers. The greatest batsman in the history of the game, Sir Donald Bradman (1998), says

" I am all in favour of the batsman starting to lift his bat and making preliminary movement with his feet before the ball is delivered. It saves a Precious fraction of a Second and appears to serve the same purpose as the preliminary waggle before starting your swing in golf."

Sir Garfield Sobers, often considered the batsman second only to Bradman in terms of ability, also states that the preliminary movement is like the golf waggle. However, he goes further and believes that this natural reflex can be conditioned according to the type of bowling encountered. Against fast bowling, he suggest that the back foot should move 12-14 cm back and across towards the off stump just before the ball is released. At the same time the bat should lift a corresponding distance. The theory behind this is to give the batter a little extra time to sight the ball, and prevent any large preliminary movement of the front foot, which would inhibit back foot play if the ball is pitched short. Against medium pace and spin bowling Sir Garfield argues that the initial movement can be slightly forward as much of this bowling is played on the front foot, and the batter would have more time to play back if it is pitched short. This is a rational attempt to optimise the initial movement and it shows that elite players recognise the value in doing this. It is not just an abstract ideal proposed by biomechanics! In fact, there are innumerable examples of Test players who believe in the necessity of optimising the initial movement - Sunil Gavaskar, Greg Chappell, Ian Chappell. Bob Woolmer, and Imran Khan - just to name a few.

Bob Woolmer (1995) has a slightly different perspective on the initial movement. He believes that the initial movement is used to establish a rhythm, which makes it easier to move the feet against fast bowling. He states that there are three main ways in which this rhythm is generated: a back foot movement, a front foot movement, or a double movement (e.g. when the back foot and front foot move wider before release). Unfortunately, there is no explanation as to what this rhythm initiates and why it enhances footwork.

It is apparent that the execution and timing of the initial movement is critical to batting performance. However, what are the mechanical principles behind the initial movement can they be optimised? The simple back and across initial movement is rarely used today in its pure form. From our experience as coaches, many cricketers have said that they feel out of balance when they use the simple back foot initial movement, and find it difficult to move forwards. Therefore they often combine this with a front foot movement, making it a double movement). Unfortunately. This sometimes moves the batter's legs well in front of the wicket, increasing the susceptibility to an lbw decision. Also, in many cases this movement does not improve a player's ability to play back because the front foot moves last, having therefore the same consequences as a front foot moves last, having therefore the same consequences as a front foot initial movement. Many young cricketers today also use the pure front foot movement. Apparently this is more natural, and they feel comfortable with it. However, it can seriously compromise their ability to play back against quality fast bowling.

The initial movement seems an unresolved issue in cricket technique. There are many schools of thought. However, none seem to be entirely satisfactory. This is to be expected. The initial movement is a largely unconscious movement that incorporates the synchronisation of many different muscles in a fraction of a second. So is there any point in inquiring any further? Should it be just considered a natural phenomenon? The problem with accepting this latter position is that the coach would be unable to improve any gifted young batter who has an inappropriate initial movement to fast bowling, seriously affecting the ability to negotiate a fast short-pitched delivery? Accept if or change it? And more significantly change it to what?

The Ranjitsinhji Principle

After years of research, and much debate, a major discovery was found in the pages of the classic book by K.S. Ranjitsinhji. The Jubilee book of Cricket. William Blackheart and Sons. London. 1897. Kumar Shri Ranjitsinhji, who represented England in Test cricket, is considered the major exponent of style in the Golden Age of cricket. His contemporaries could only describe him as a genius. And his name is often linked with the names of past great players: W.G. Grace. Victor Trumper, and even sir Donald Bradman. Here is a short account C.B. Fry (1905) in an assessment of his abilities:

"There are many batsmen who make some one stroke with such wonderful ease and effect that all their other strokes receive in comparison but scant appreciation. In Ranjitsinhji's case every turn of his bat has this appearance of extreme facility, to such a degree, indeed, that his style seems almost casual or careless.

The distinctive trait of his cricket is an electric quickness both in the conception and execution of his strokes. Thereby he differs from the run of batsmen in that he judges the flight of the ball about half as soon again, and can therefore shape for his strokes more readily and with more certainty. At the same time he need not, owing to his marvelous rapidity of movement, allow himself as much margin for error as others find necessary: and it is this quickness that enables him to take, even an the fastest of wickets, the most unheard-of liberties without fatal results."

In an era of uncovered pitches, he scored for Sussex from 1895 to 1908 more than 17,000 runs at an average exceeding 65 (Parker, 1975). Why was Ranji, as he was affectionately known, so much superior to his contemporaries? Obviously, a supernatural ability had something to do with it. But was there any technique that gave him an advantage? He was always reported to have had the most brilliant of footwork, so it reasonable to deduce that he had an efficient initial movement. There is only one filmstrip of Ranji batting, but nothing could be revealed here because he was only hitting some casual warm-up strokes. However, it is a great fortune that Ranji described his preliminary movement strategy in his book:

"There is a difference of opinion as to whether a player should stand with his weight equally distributed an both legs, or let all of it fall upon the right leg. I think the weight should be almost entirely upon the right leg."

Further information can be gleaned from Great batsmen. Their methods at a glance by C.B. Fry and G.W. Beldam. In this book there are a series of still photographs that give a good account of how Ranji played. There are photographs of his stance, and most importantly, position during the initial movement. His stance was balanced with the feet close together, and the front foot pointing to cover. The rear foot was probably pointed just backward of point. In the next photograph, Ranji adopted his characteristic initial position, which will from now on be referred to as the "Ranji position ". A significant portion of the weight was thrown onto the ball of the back foot, which was also turned slightly so that it pointed slightly in front of the batting crease. Bending at the hips helped move the head forwards, and the bat was lifted to about shoulder height primarily by the lifting action of the wrists. This is an accurate depiction of Ranji's initial movement. However the question must be asked: "Is the Ranji position mechanically useful?" This is an important point of inquiry. It is entirely possible that the Ranji position is merely an elaborate stylistic embellishment, or a position of comfort that would not confer any mechanical advantages to a batter at all.

To investigate the mechanics behind the Ranji position, we used a qualitative optimisation modelling approach:

Qualitative Optimisation Analysis: Ranji Position

Required Output: Initial position that optimises ability to move back and forward, and execute efficient stroke play.

Cost Function: Time to execute stroke.

Design Variables:

1. More weight on rear foot

2. Head moved forwards

3. Bend of the hips

4. Shoulders and hips approximately aligned from wicket to wicket

5. Wrist-lift of the bat

Constraints:

1. Head behind the ball with two-eyes almost parallel

2. Vertical bat during stroke

The qualitative model captures the essential features of the Ranji movement, and places them in a biomechanical context. To adopt the Ranji position with weight on the rear foot and head forward, the right pelvis must be shifted backwards and laterally rotated to the right (for right hand batter) With the weight predominantly on the rear foot, front foot movement is made very much more efficient. The great Ranji says, "It is worth noticing that in every kind of exercise where the legs are used the leg which it is necessary to move forward ought not to have any weight upon it at the time of being moved" This is very sound biomechanics. In this position, a torque can be easily applied about the pelvis's center of rotation to lift the front foot. However, Ranji goes further and suggests that alternative methods of moving forward are inefficient: "If a man stands with much weight on his left leg he has to transfer the weight to his right leg before making a forward stroke, if he is to make the stroke without overbalancing himself." This argument holds just as true for batters who have the weight evenly distributed on both feet - some weight has to be transferred to the back foot before the front one is moved. Certainly, the method prescribed by Ranji is more efficient, and saves time: it partially minimises the cost function, and so is a step in the right direction.

The Ranji position has been shown to make front-foot movement quicker. However, we are interested in an initial position that optimises both front and back foot movements. Can the argument for extra weight on the back foot to improve front foot play be applied in reverse to conclude that back foot play would be made more difficult? Ranji had experimented with his method for a long time and had this to say in reply: "It is a curious thing that by keeping the weight on the right leg a player can move forward more readily than from the alternative position, and yet he can move back wards if he wishes to do so without the slightest difficulty. That is to say, the position recommended facilitates forward- playing, and is no hindrance in playing back or cutting" Now Ranji is making definite claims that his initial position is an optimal one! Interestingly, a simple treatment of mechanics seems to supports Ranji's claim. The Ranji position forms a characteristic C-shape. When the body is in this configuration, the head is in front of the body's center of mass. The position of the center of mass is not constant; it varies with the configuration of the body. In the Ranji position, the center of mass is not constant; it varies with the configuration of the body. In the Ranji position, the center of mass may move slightly forward from its position when the body is stationary but it is still behind the position of the head. The importance of this cannot be overemphasised, because in the Ranji position there is more weight on the rear foot, which means that weight has to be transferred to the front foot before the back foot is moved. Normally, this would mean that the ability to play back has been diminished. However, if the head is moved slightly downwards in conjunction with a right lateral pelvic rotation, weight can be quickly applied to the front foot. Effectively this movement generates a couple about the pelvis's center of rotation, which slightly elevates the hips, and lifts the back foot. The secret lies in the position in the head. If the head is behind or even in line with the body's center of mass, then the act of reloading weight onto the front foot becomes more difficult, and time consuming. Also the position of the center of mass with respect to the virtual center of pelvis rotation is important.

The Ranjitsinhji principle is a very strong candidate for an optimal solution to the initial movement which involve a different weight, distribution strategy, the Ranji position appears superior. It optimises the ability to play forward without diminishing the ability to play forward without diminishing the ability to play back. In fact, it appears to improve the ability to back. In an era of cricket when fast bowling can dominate cricket matches, this is indeed a practical principle. It definitely appears that K.S. Ranjitsinhji did achieve a considerable advantage over his contemporaries by using this method.

What has been discussed so far about the Ranjitsinhji principle satisfies part of requirements for an optimal solution - it has optimized the ability to move forward & back. In this way, the cost function (i.e. the time to execute the stroke) has been partially minimized. Yet there are other considerations that would have an effect on the cost function, such as back lift. Recall that the qualitative model for the Ranji position also specifies efficient stroke making as a required output. The initial movement cannot be considered separately from the rest of stroke making. There has to be a unity that binds the separate facets of technique into one smooth process. Therefore, there is still more to be considered before we can claim that the Ranjitsinhji principle forms the foundation of elite batting.

Modernising the Ranjitsinhji Principle

However brilliant K.S. Ranjitsinhji was, it is unlikely that his style of batting would be as effective today without some modification. Bowling is faster these days, and fast bowlers can often operate in tandem for much longer than they did in the past. Also, pitches are different. The pitches in Australian are generally fast, and this encourages the strategy of persistent short pitch bowling. It should be no surprise therefore if we fashion the Ranjitsinhji principle to cater for the modern climate.

The Ranjitsinhji principle in its pure form optimises the movements forward and back. In the modern game, it is necessary to move back and across. Though Ranjitsinhji himself did this better than his contemporaries, the principle can be further adapted to perform this task more efficiently Rather than merely adopt the Ranji position one can move slightly back and across before placing more weight on the back foot while ensuring that the head is kept forwards. Therefor, the Ranji position is adopted in the same way as before, but now with the rear foot about 15-30 cm back and towards the off-stump. This gives several advantages. First, it gives the batter a good indication of the position of the off stump. With the modern emphasis of bowling in a channel on and just outside off stump, a batter must have some means of knowing when to let to ball pass to the wicket keeper. Second, the batter is already in a partial back foot position. Short-pitched fast bowling is the norm today. Therefore, it pays to be biased towards the back foot position before the ball is delivered. From this position, the batter can move further back if the ball is short without compromising the ability to move forward if the ball is pitched up, because there is extra weight placed on the back foot. Third for most deliveries that are played on the front foot, the front leg has to travel slightly to the left of the line of the ball. By moving back and across, the front foot is inside the line of the back foot. This tends to minimise the effect of the front foot moving too early, which usually results in the front foot moving outside the line of the back foot, and unless the ball is pitched on off stump or wider, causes the batter to play across the front pad. This increases the likelihood of an lbw dismissal. Fourth, in the modern Ranji position the batter is in a more balanced position because the area of base support is increased. Fifth, leg-side play is enhanced because the front foot is on the left side of the back foot, providing the ideal position from which to play balls on or around leg stump. And finally, the elevated hip line (right lateral pelvic rotation) is a source of stored energy, which can be released during the downswing to generate bat speed.

2

PERPENDICULAR BAT STROKES

Defensive Play

Before proceeding with an analysis of back foot defensive play, two questions need to be considered: "What is the purposes of playing back? What is the method of playing back?" Typical responses to the first question revolve around giving the batter more time to play the ball, or putting the batter into a more favorable position to control a ball that is rising above waist level. Such comments are reasonably close to the mark. However, when it comes to the second question, there are few cricketers, and coaches for that matter that describe the process accurately. The classical text book method stipulates that in response to a short ball the back foot should move a good distance back and across toward the off stump under the eyes. Generally, this same method is prescribed for all short pitch deliveries irrespective of the line of the ball. However, some texts add that for a ball on the leg stump the front leg should be drawn backwards as the stroke is executed. Yet other state that for such leg stump short deliveries the back foot should positioned in line with middle or even leg stump. Both these methods stipulate that the back foot must still remain parallel with the batting crease.

Before showings deficiencies in the classical method, it is important to point out that it is one thing for a cricketer to be able to be able to execute an efficient back foot defensive stroke against a fast bowler, and quite another to understand or describe the processes that enable him/her to do this. It is therefore common to hear even strong back foot players giving an inadequate account of the back foot defensive technique. This situation can be avoided if one thinks in terms of biomechanical optimization. A basic qualitative schema is shown below.

Qualitative Optimisation Analysis: Back Foot Defensive Strokes

Required Output: Hit ball with bat on back foot.

Cost Function: Time to execute stroke.

Design Variables:

1. Initial position - Modern Ranji Position
2. Bat downswing
3. Back foot movement
4. Front foot movement

5. Weight transfer

Constraints:

1. Head behind the ball with two-eyes almost parallel

2. Vertical bat during stroke

In the preceding sections, the Ranji position was shown to optimise a batter's ability to move forward and back. Therefore, we now make it a compulsory part of all the basic strokes as it precedes the release of the ball. Therefore, a description of the process of playing black begins from the Ranji position: bat at waist height, weight on back foot, head forward, and hips laterally retired to the right (rh bat). For the purposes of this discussion, consider that the ball is not only short, but also bowled at 90 miles per hour, which is fast becoming the common speed of an elite Test fast bowler. Therefore, the batter should execute the back foot defensive stroke by first of all minimising the cost function, which represents the time required to implement the stroke. This should particularly be the case when the ball is delivered at speeds in excess of 70 miles per hour.

The primary aim of the batter is to successfully defend such a ball. The optimal technique should clearly be directed towards minimising the cost function. It does not make sense, therefore, to employ high back lifts, particularly those that involve a significant lifting of the shoulders. The further the bat is lifted, the further it must come down to meet the ball resulting in a hurried stroke at best. Also, if the ball should possess some swing or cut, then a successful result is unlikely. For defensive play there is no need to optimise bat speed, so a high back lift is not necessary. It will be shown later that there are other ways of increasing bat speed when required. For the moment, a back lift activated primarily by the wrists to the level of the waist will suffice.

Another feature of inefficient back foot defensive play is what elite coaches call "The second back lift" Such a lift is initiated when a batter has preliminarily lifted the bat to some height, but then again lifts the bat with the arms some significant time (lift threshold time) after the ball has left the bowler's hand. The value of this lift threshold time varies among batters, and also depends on the ball release speed, but its reality is often evident in batters that consistently misting the ball by making late ball contact. From the point of view of the cost function, any such secondary lift wastes precious fractions of a second, as this detracts from the time available to execute the stroke. On the contrary, elite batters tend to synchronies the end of their back lifts with the moment of ball release, so that once the ball is in flight, they are only concentrating on bringing the bat down to meet the ball. Clearly, this strategy means that the bat has less distance to travel before meeting the ball once it has left the bowler's hand, and therefore the stroke can be executed with less bat speed, which gives the batter more control over the defensive stroke.

The particular qualitative optimisation approach that is being used here is termed end effecter optimisation. By starting with the end-effecter, which is the bat in this case, it was logically determined that after ball release, the batter should be primarily concerned with, bringing the bat towards the ball, and so the timing of the back lift is important. Also, high back lifts, particularly those activated without the use of the wrists, can only make it more difficult to play defensively.

The first step established, namely that of the back lift, we now seeked optimal solutions progressively further back in the kinetic chain, and checked whether these local optimal solutions are part of the optimal solution for the whole movement (e.g. global optimal solution). Therefore, we needed to consider how to optimally combine the back foot movement (i.e. back and across movement) with the downswing with the bat. Clearly, the back foot cannot move after the downswing. Otherwise, the footwork would be initiated after the stroke had been completed. Also the back foot cannot move before the downswing because the bat is elevated, and this movement would cause the bat to synchronies the downswing because the bat is elevated, and this movement would cause the bat to move outwards to a position in line with gully or point. There is only one alternative left, and that is to synchronise the downswing of the bat with the movement of the back foot as it moves towards the off stump. The process would be completed when the front foot comes to rest alongside the back foot.

What we have come up with so far then is an exceedingly simple and efficient method of playing a back foot defensive stroke. The batter has to merely step behind the bat! This is the purpose of playing back - to step behind the bat. While stepping behind the bat, if the bat is brought down and towards the ball, then it is clearly evident that the cost function has been minimised. The stroke is executed quickly and with a minimum of effort. Even against the fastest bowlers, a batter using this technique, (probably the most notable example was sir Garfield Sobers), has sufficient time to execute the stroke. This "stepping behind the bat technique" also shows why it is inefficient to play a back foot defensive stroke with a high back lift. It is only possible to begin the process of stepping behind the bat when it is at about waist height. Therefore, for a back lift around shoulder height, the bat must travel down to the level of the waists before the back foot can start moving back and across. Against fast bowlers there is insufficient time to do this, so the batter will usually be late on the stroke and contact the ball beside the body. In fact, there is often no time to move the back foot across at all. It could remain on the line of middle or even leg stump, preventing the eyes from being positioned behind the line of the ball. Contrast this with the optimal back foot defensive stroke, and it is clearly evident which one is superior. To complete the optimal analysis, consider the constraint conditions that of the vertical bat, and eyes behind the ball. The need to satisfy these conditions may seem obvious; however, several coaches insist that the ball should be struck under the eyes with the bat beside the body. This defies common sense. The eyes are in front of the head, and like most primates, humans have stereoscopic vision, so it makes sense to hit the ball in front of the eyes. If the ball is hit in front of the eyes then the batter can more or less track the ball all the way onto the bat. However, if it is hit under the eyes, then the eyes have to use two distinct tracking strategies to pick up the trajectory of the ball. First the eyes look forward as the ball travels towards the batter, but then this tracking has to be abruptly interrupted, as the head has to look downwards to prepare for contact beneath the eyes. There is a crucial period of time when the eyes have either lost vision of the ball or are moving quickly into another tracking position. It is virtually impossible to negotiate any late movement or unpredictable bounce using this method. Clearly, having the eyes behind the trajectory of the ball for as long as possible gives a significant advantage.

There is one further reason why the eyes need to behind the ball - weight transference! In all strokes, even defensive ones, it is desirable to have the body's momentum transferred into the ball. By making ball contact in front of the eyes (constraint) with a vertical bat (constraint) then the weight is naturally transferred forwards (design variable no. 5) in the direction of the intended stroke. This is important not only when it comes to supplying power to the back foot drives, but also for pushing for one's and two's , which is also an integral part of defensive play.

Side On vs Front On

Now what about the classical method's insistence that the rear foot run parallei to the batting crease, and that the body be perfectly side on for all the back foot strokes, irrespective of the line of the ball. This has been an issue subject to much discussion in recent years. Let's first hear what the two greatest cricketers of the world (i.e. Bradman and Sobers) have to say on the matter.

"Some coaches advocate that the toes remain parallel with the popping crease - others that they should point partially towards the bowler. I favour the happy medium and think it best for the toes to be pointing rather towards cover or mid off." - Bradman (1958)

"Some coaches advocate that the toes remain parallel with the popping crease others that they should point partially towards the bowler. I favour the latter with the front one falling into place alongside." -Bradman (1998)

"There is not one back foot defensive shot technique, though many coaches and manuals dictate there is. The technique for a ball outside off stump is to keep the body mostly side on which is completely different to the chest on toes pointing to the bowler technique, employed when the ball is on the middle stump." - Sobers (1985)

It apparent that Bradman and sobers are firmly of the opinion that the rear toe needs to open up towards cover or even straighter when the need arises (). The insistence that the back foot remain parallel to the batting crease for all back foot strokes is difficult to justify. The aim of the back foot stroke is to step behind the bat so that the eyes and body are behind the ball. For instance, if the ball has pitched in line with the leg stump then it is not possible, or extremely difficult to pull the bat in seafront of the body if the back foot is parallel to the batting crease. There is plenty of video and photographical evidence that elite batsmen of the past and those of today play such balls on the back foot from open hipped position. Weather it is K.S. Ranjitsinhji, Sir Donald Bradman, Sir Garfield Sobers, Ian Chappel or Sachin Tendulkar short balls in line with stumps are played in non classical open hipped positions with the bat out in front of the eyes. Of course, it must be said that for balls on or out side the off stump these batsmen would revert to the side on position.

One reason for the almost dogmatic insistence that all back foot strokes be played from a fully side on position is that the past were not aware of the optimal process of stepping behind the bat. They thought that to open up would cause the bat to come down from near the gully direction. Therefore, they specified that the batter stand beside the ball and swing the bat straight down like a pendulum. They also believed that it was only possible to play a back foot drive from a side on position. However, if the batter steps behind the bat in the correct manner, an almost straight path of the bat can be maintained. Also, we will show later that it is inefficient to play most back foot drives from a pure side on position. More power can be derived when the toes are pointing in front of the batting crease. In fact many would be surprised to know that even the MCC Cricket Coaching Manual published in 1974 recognised the logical need to open up the rear foot when the ball pitched on line with the leg stump.

"...........to ball on, or just outside the leg stump and for a stroke aimed at mid on or wider, the toe will **point more** ***towards cover".*** -MCC Cricket Coaching Manual (1974)

Just a ward of caution: "It is dangerous to play short balls pitch on or outside off stump from a fully open hipped position". In this case, the open position inhibits the inside out inside out downswing of the bat required to play balls through the off side.

C.B. Fry Wrist-Action and Arm-Swing Theory

Sir Donald Bradman (1958) said that to play forcing shots off the back foot ***"demands great power from wrists and forearms, and very good timing"***. Therefore, before proceeding with the mechanics of the back foot drive, it is necessary to investigate the mechanics of wrist action and see how this can be combined with arm-swing.

A very important principle in this area was conceptualised by Charles Burgess Fry, who was born in 1872 in Surrey and played 26 matches for England in the era of K.S. Ranjitsinhji. C.B. Fry was somewhat of an enigmatic character. A first-class honours graduate in Classical moderations, he won his blue in all four years at Oxford and also won blues for soccer and athletics. It was generally believed that he would have played many more matches for England if he had the time. A natural athlete he held the world long jump record for 21 years! C.B. Fry was a correct batsman and a great thinker on the game. He performed two monumental works in the early 1900s based on the classic still action photography of G.W. Beldam: Great Bawlers and Fielders: their Methods at a Glance (Macmillan & Co. Ltd. New York, 1906) and Great Batsmen: Their Methods at a Glance (Macmillan & Co. Ltd., New York, 1908) These are the first biomechanical studies in cricket, and should be part of every coach's library. Even though many of the techniques described are dated or obsolete, it clearly demonstrates C.B. Fry's keen sense of analysis, and identifies many fundamental technical problems that are still relevant today.

So what has the great C.B. Fry to say on wrist work? In his classic text, Cricket (Batsmanship). Eveleigh Nash Co. Ltd, London, 1912., he accurately describes the modern back lift with cocked wrists:

"If your bat is grounded face full towards the bowler, and you lift it back with out longitudinal turn of the arms. The face is full towards the ground when the bat is extended out behind you. But if you lift it back with longitudinal turn, its face, when the bat is away out behind you is turned flush towards point. This turn of the arms, combined with pure wrist work as described above, enables you to whirl a bat round in a small circle, of which your wrists are the centre. It is this combination of pure wrist work with longitudinal arm turn that is what is really meant when we talk of wrist in such a stroke as a Drive."

Here C.B. Fry has described accurately the mechanics of the ideal back lift, which uses the movement of the wrists. He differentiates between pure wrist work which is only flexion-extension of the wrist, and longitudinal arm-turn, which is a turn of the forearm about its longitudinal axis. What is known as wrist work in modern cricket is really the combination of these two processes. So by bending the elbows and lifting the bat to waist height with the wrists cocked the batter waits for the ball in the Ranji position.

The next stage is the downswing of the bat. To understand what C.B. Fry says about this it is necessary to first define some terms. Half-arm-swing (or short swing) is defined as the flexion/ extension of the elbows with pure wrist work and longitudinal arm work while the upper arms remain close to the side. Full length arm swing (or long swing) is the swing of the full arm from the shoulders with no elbow action or wrist work. C.B. Fry considers the optimum downswing of the cricket bat to consist of a short swing followed by a long swing.

"The advantages of a short swing during the first half of the stroke and the long one during the second are these: the short swing can bring the bat down to the intended point of impact with the ball faster, consequently the stroke need not be begun so soon consequently you have longer time to judge the flight of the ball; consequently you are likely to time it better. Moreover, the effort of half-arm swing being less that of full length arm-swing, the poise of the body is less likely to be disturbed an important point. It is

well known that players who hit with full arm swing in the first half of the stroke arm liable to pull this because the swing of the arms at full length is liable to throw the upper part of the body away from the line of the stroke, just as a hammer thrower is overbalanced at the end of his whirl. But a full swing in the second half of the stroke is good because in any follow through freedom and length make for power."

This gives clear insight into the mechanics of obtaining power from the downswing while minimising the cost function - i.e. to reduce the time to execute the stroke. Initiating the downswing with mainly wrist action certainly means that the bat can be accelerated quickly to meet the ball in front of the eyes. The faster the delivery the more important the half-arm-swing becomes. Remember, that if contact is made in front of the eyes then the weight can be fully transferred into the stroke. There is little point of a long downswing if contact is made under the eyes: apart from not achieving a position to track the ball optimally, the body weight would not be fully transferred into the stroke. From a mechanical point of view, the full dynamics behind the short swing is complex because it is not a pure action. For instance, there is some pulling of the shoulders forward before the forearms are extended.

However, in simple terms, the effective moment arm of the coupled forearms to its virtual pivot point (approximately half- way between the elbows) during the short swing is almost half as long as the effective moment arm of the combined whole arm mechanism to its virtual pivot point (approximately half way between the glenohumeral joints) during the long swing. Therefore, the action of the short swing is significantly quicker. Also consider one additional point. The short swing makes up for some lack of swing distance compared to the long swing in that it travels further forward than the long swing because there is time for the bat to make contact with the ball in front of the eyes: whereas if the long swing is used exclusively, it would be a major effort to even make ball contact under the eyes. So the lack in angular sweep of the short swing is less than first supposed.

So far we have established the advantages of the making a short swing to the point of ball contact. What happens beyond this? Let's see what C.B. Fry has to say:

"The bat should meet the ball at the bottom of the swing. Then the bat should be allowed to go right through to the full length of the arms, so that in the second half of the stroke (i.e. in the following through part after impact) there is full

length arm swing plus half arm swing plus the half-arm-swing, plus the finish of the pure wrist work plus the finish of the longitudinal or axial arm turn, plus the finish of the finger pressure, or accelerating change of grip................a full swing in the second half of the stroke is good because in any follow-through freedom and length make for power."

What C.B. Fry is talking about here is really quite profound and describes how wrist and arm action are combined for most of the attacking shots. After the half arm swing has ended the elbows are extended to their optimal angle and the bat makes approximately a 90 degree angle with the bottom forearm. The wrists should be at maximum velocity, as contact with the ball is imminent. If the batter uses a standard batting grip, then is not possible to extend the wrists much further without doing damage to the ligaments. Therefore, in most cases, batters drastically reduce the extension rate of the wrists (hand angular velocity) just prior to impact at the end of the half-swing, and as a result lose significant bat speed. There seems to have been no point in using the wrists in the first place. But, there is an alternative way of maintaining hand angular velocity, and that is to accelerate the arms during (or slightly before) ball contact. If this is performed correctly, then the hands can reach a high angular velocity at impact, because the accelerating arms will exert a force at the wrist joints that would naturally inhibit the hands from extending (Newton's Third Law). In this way the batter can concentrate on extending the wrists as fast as possible during the half-swing with the knowledge that the full length-arm-swing will not permit the hands to extend beyond their natural limit. Therefore, there is a bat speed transition phase; first bat speed is generated by the extension of the wrists (hand angular velocity); then at about ball contact, the linear velocity of the wrist joints maintains bat speed during the full length arm swing. It is unlikely that C.B. Fry knew the exact mechanics behind what he suggested. However, he made a significant discovery based on his experience. We can now proceed to the mechanics of the back foot drive.

Back Foot Drives

The back foot stroke so far described requires the batter to step behind the bat by moving the rear foot back and across towards the off stump while simultaneously bringing the bat down to make contact with the ball in front of the eyes. This process very similar for the back foot drive, except that now more power must be applied to the stroke, and therefore the batter must generate sufficient bat speed at ball contact. In the preceding section, we described how arm swing and wrist action are combined to generate bat speed. However, there is more to back foot driving than merely this. In fact, there is a principle that lies at the very core of effective back foot driving it is the Ranjitsinjhi principle!

The amazing feature of the Ranjitsinhsji principle is that it not only optimises a batter's ability to move forward and back, but also aids in the generation of power. Recall that when a batter is in the Ranji position there is a significant right lateral rotation and shift of the pelvis to the right (rh batter). Therefore, when the batter needs to play a back foot drive, the pelvis can be quickly shifted to the left (i.e. forwards). This action would accelerate the shoulders forwards, and enable the forearms and wrists to accelerate towards the ball (i.e. during C.B. Fry's half-arm-swing). Then, after contact, a full- arm swing can complete the follow-thorough

First generates tremendous power off the back foot by combining a lateral forward shift of the hips with the half-arm swing and full length arm swing cycle. The Ranji position helps load the hips during the back foot movement prior to the downswing of the bat. Note that only a short

barely higher than that for a defensive stroke. This means that this stroke can be used against the fastest bowlers by merely extending a back foot defensive stroke! It is clear then that the prescribed method is practical, and can significantly contribute to batter's run making ability.

It is evident then that the secret in supplying power to the back foot strokes lies in the correct use of the hips. This ability is enhanced if the batter begins his stroke from the Ranji position. The hip action initiates a set of reaction forces that serve to accelerate the bat during its downswing. However, the process of coordinating this with back foot movement, front foot movement, arm swing, wrist action and ball contact is complex; and one that has not been described in the cricket literature before. This is mainly because hip action has never been identified as a mechanical characteristic of back foot driving. As a result, there are few batters that can consistently hit back foot drives straight down the wicket. In fact, throughout cricket histories there have been only a few who could do this. The greatest back foot drivers (and this should be of no surprise) were Sir Donald Bradman and Sir Garfield sobers. However others such as Viv Richards and Norman O'Neil could also be devastatingly powerful off the back foot straight down the wicket. But Bradman and sobers made back foot driving a real art. Both these players made significant use of lateral hip shift and rotation to transfer momentum into their back foot drives. Sobers even had the ability to hit back foot sixes straight over the sight screen!

An important note about optimising power for the back foot drive: the back foot must not run parallel to the crease! This is another reason why the adherence to the classical side on back foot position limits a batter's capabilities. Anatomically, for a right-hand batter, a more efficient lateral hip shift can be achieved if the back foot points towards cover point or straighter.

Below is a sequential account of the biomechanics of an optimal back foot drive (right hand batter).

Important Notes:

1: For the back foot off drives the rear foot can point anywhere between cover point and mid off. Though the bat comes down from beside the body, for the straights off drives, contact can still be made in front of the body

2: For the back foot straight drive, the rear foot can point from mid off to straight down the wicket. The batter must play this shot from beside

the ball to allow the bat to come through with force. Contact is made beside the body, but with head and eyes still behind the line of the ball. For optimal power and control for a back foot straight drive the rear foot should point towards mid off or even straighter. There can be more use of the bottom hand during the contact phase of this stroke.

3: For the back foot on drive, the rear foot can point from mid off to straight down the wicket. The batter must play this shot from beside the ball to allow the bat to come through with force. The batter is completely chest on to the ball to ensure that there is room to hit the ball to leg side. The front leg draws back further past and wide of the rear foot so that the batter can take the leading side out of the way, which would otherwise block the shot. Power is generated largely through the action of the forearms and wrists. Which roll through the ball as in a golf drive.

This particular description of the back foot drives is not found in any of the orthodox coaching literature. This may be a reason why there are few players in world cricket today that can hit back foot drives straight down the wicket for 4's or 6's. There are many players who can hit a back foot cover drive, but this is a kind of hybrid stroke between a cut and a drive, and often executed with the bat angled at 45 degrees. This stroke can be played from the orthodox side on position, as it requires little lateral hip shift.

The back foot lofted off drive is played by driving the hips forward. It is more difficult to shift the hips forward when the back foot points towards point. Hence, the author has his back foot pointing in front of point, and thrusts his rear hip forward to accelerate the bat on the downswing. This stroke cannot be hit as powerfully as the back foot straight or on drives, because hip actio is inhibited by the constraint that the shoulders rotate through the line of the ball. The back foot cover drive can be successfully executed with a rolling action of the wrists, because the ball is hit beside the body with a semi perpendicular bat. It is the easiest of the back foot drives.

One reason why the traditional literature, and previous qualitative biomechanical analyses of back foot driving have suggested the side on approach, stems from the theory that the rotation of the shoulder girdle is primarily responsible for the power and direction of the drives. Following this line of argument, if the hips are open, then the shoulder line does not run parallel to the intended direction of the stroke, so power and diction would be difficult to achieve. Unfortunately, adherents of this theory do not realise that the rotation of the shoulder girdle by itself cannot supply much power to the hips before power can be generated. Shoulder girdle rotation is actually secondary to the lateral hip shift when it comes to delivering power to a drive. As such, it is important for the body to move into a position that optimises the lateral hip shift rather than shoulder girdle rotation rate. The upper body is not composed of solid inflexible rigid segments, so the trunk, shoulders, arms and wrists can easily be manipulated with practice to hit a ball in a direction that does not run strictly parallel to the shoulder line.

By following the procedures mentioned here, and perhaps some coaching from the likes of Sir Garfield sobers (West Indies) or Owen Mottau (Sri Lanka), there is no reason why a reasonably gifted batter cannot make these back foot drives part of the repertoire, and greatly increase his/her run-making capability, and rate of scoring!

Defensive Play

For deliveries pitched too full to play back to and too short to drive, the forward defensive shot is used. The same qualitative approach that optimised for back foot defensive play is equally applicable here so there is no need to repeat the process. The same cost function is used namely to minimise time spent executing the shot. Therefore, the bat is only lifted to about waist height, and brought down when the ball has been released. The bat is brought down to meet the ball in front of the eyes, while the hips are laterally shifted forwards. The bat passes close to the pad, so there is little gap between them, and the body weight transferred into the stroke. Because ball contact is made in front of the eyes, the front foot must land behind the line of the ball, so that the ball can be hit slightly in front of the pad. To ensure that the bat travels behind the line of thew ball, the front foot is pointed to extra-cover, and the bat brought down over the instep. The advantage of hitting in front of the eyes, apart from the fact that the eyes can track the ball more effectively, is that the weight can be more effectively transferred into the stroke. This is important, as in many defensive strokes, particularly in the presence of close-in catchers, it is important to keep the ball), the front knee is bent, and the back foot lifted and turned towards the line of the intended stroke.

The front foot defensive stroke. Critical features are bat in front of the pad, bent front

knee, foot pointing towards the off side and rear foot lifted and turned after contact.

Playing the front foot defensive stroke from the Ranji position. The position creates a solid platform from which to move forward, and enhances the ability to transfer weight into the stroke while maintaining the eyes behind the line of the ball. Note that point of ball contact is well in front of the pad.

What has been described is the optimal method of playing the forward defensive strokes, according to some very simple principles. The result is a very simple and effective stroke that has been used by all elite batters throughout the ages. It is difficult to imagine how it could be played differently. However, the orthodox method departs quite significantly from the optimal method we have outlined. It generally specifies that a large step be taken with the front foot placed beside the line of the ball., sop that contact can be made behind the front pad. Also, in many texts, the lifting and turning of the rear foot is discouraged. They often talk about the importance of forming a solid base of support, and therefore suggest that the rear foot be firmly planted on the ground. However, it is unnatural to have the rear foot forcible pegged to the ground. It does not allow for weight transference into the stroke, and encourages late ball contact behind the front leg, particularly off a large step is taken. It is also a more difficult position in which to contender a seaming or spinning ball and greatly inhibits the batter's ability to work the ball for one's and two's if the need arises the batter is committed to a defensive stroke. In addition, it is more difficult to track a swinging ball, as the eyes have to first look up at the ball during the first there quarters of the ball's flight, and then look down quickly to a position behind the front leg where ball contact is anticipated. It is virtually impossible to track the ball during this latter stage of flight. This process minimises the margin for error, as contact must be made at a particular point in space beside and behind the front leg. However, if the batter intends to make contact in front of the leg, then no such fixed contact point is defined. To counter a moving ball, the batter can position his bat anywhere in front of the pad, and even pull the bat away if required. For instance, if the ball swings in late after the front foot has been planted, then the batter can play slightly in front and across the pad. In the orthodox case, the batter would have been struck on the pad. If the ball moves towards the slips, the batter has the freedom to even play slightly away from the front leg and open the bat face to play the ball on the off side.

Alternatively, the batter can drop the bat on the inside of the ball's flight path and let the ball travel unimpeded to the wicket keeper. In the orthodox case, an edge may have resulted. Similar arguments can be used for the case of the spinning ball.

The orthodox front foot defensive stroke. Note how contact is made behind the front pad, the ball struck under the eyes, and the weight not transferred down into the ball because the rear foot is pegged to the ground. Such a position is unsuitable to counter the moving ball and lends itself to lbw's. Furthermore, the batter is not looking at the ball during the crucial latter part of the ball's flight. The orthodox technique is even prescribed for strokes on the on side!

A forward defensive push through the off side. Freeze the frames during and just after contact, and observe how it differs from the previous video of the orthodox defensive stroke. The weight is fully transferred into the ball, and batsman is fully in control of the stroke.

The other aspect that is incorrectly specified or omitted in the orthodox method is the importance of front foot orientation. For a defensive stroke, in particular, a constraint is that the bat should be, as much as possible, behind or outside the line of the ball at impact. The traditional methods of front foot defensive play do not address this all important issue. For it is this that more often than not determines the fate of a batter's innings there is little point in having all the strokes and a good-looking defence, if the batter is susceptible to edging deliveries to the slips. That is why the insistence that the front foot point in the direction of the intended stroke is difficult to justify. With such a foot orientation it is natural to track the ball to the left of the ball's flight path especially if contact is made behind the front leg! Therefore, for a ball pitched on middle and off and drifting away to slips, the batter who intends to play this ball in the orthodox manner with the front toe pointing straight down the wicket will make contact with this ball on the outside half of the bat. Edges are likely to result from this practice. However, if the front foot is pointing towards cover, then it much easier to move the front foot across so that it is slightly outside the line of the oncoming ball. Then the bat is already in a partial position to cover for any away movement. Basically, if the front foot points towards about extra cover, then it is more natural to play slightly to the right of the ball's flight path, so that contact can be made with the full face of the bat. A similar argument holds for the optimal method of countering leg-spin bowling off the front foot. The greatest batters have used this strategy.

Finally, a word on playing deliveries that pitch on middle and leg stump. This is one area that really shows up the novice coaches. It is absolutely critical that for the front foot strokes through the on-side the front foot remains pointed towards the off-side. This foot orientation makes it natural to place the foot behind the line of the ball, and play the stroke over the instep, not alongside it. Using this technique, the pad acts as a second line of defence, which is necessary because these strokes are played across the line of the ball.

The front foot defensive stroke on the on side is played by taking only a small step forwards behind the line of the ball with the foot pointing to the off side. The ball is struck over the instep, as the right hip opens up. The ball is struck over the instep, as the right hip opens up, Note haw the head and eyes are right behind the handle of the bat and the line of the stroke. This is achieved by opening up the right hip during the stroke.

The traditional teaching is that the front foot point to mid on, and ball contact occur behind the front leg. In this case, the batter has no second line of defence for the on side strokes. Also, it is impractical to move the front foot to the left of the ball because the position of thew head, which is the heaviest part of the body, causes much of the weight to be distributed on the balls of the feet prior to ball release. This results in a torque that acts to tip the body towards the off side. To play any ball on the on side this torque must first be overcome, and this takes up time. In fact, it is often not possible to totally overcome this initial tipping moment. This is the reason that in one day cricket the rules are far more stringent for a leg side wide than for an off side one.

Furthermore, it goes without saying that contact is made in front of the pad. For a ball delivered over the wicket to a right hand batter, the flight path of the ball is angled towards the leg-side. In the traditional technique, the front foot is placed beside the line of this flight path, and contact predicted behind the front leg. The batter is attempting to hit across the line of the ball at a predetermined point of contact! Even if contact is made, the ball can run across the face of the bat and hit the pad. Instead, by taking a short step during the initial portion of the balls flight and opening up the hips, the batter can watch the remainder of the ball's flight and make contact with the ball at a suitable point in front of the pad. Against a left-arm over the wicket bowler (or right arm around) it is even more imperative to strike the ball in such a manner with the foot pointing towards the off, because the ball is generally moving towards the slips. Playing an on side stroke with the traditional technique opens up all the stumps, and a bowled result is likely.

Driving

The front foot drive is an extension of the defensive stroke. Many of the optimisation principles derived previously for the back foot case apply equally for the front foot. Again it is the action of the hips that generate much of the power in the stroke. The batter starts from the Ranji position and moves the front foot behind the pitch of the ball. The shoulders are pulled forwards and rotated when the hips are laterally shifted forwards. It is important that the hips and shoulders stay in line with the intended direction of the ball at this stage. The shoulder rotation initiates the downswing of the bat. Then when the shoulder motion decelerates the wrists extend rabidly until ball contact, which occurs in front of the eyes. At this point, the front knee is bent, the rear foot lifted and turned, and the weight fully transferred into the stroke. Excessive rotation of the hips is prevented because the front knee is bent, and the front foot pointed towards the front must occur to facilitate momentum transfer into the stroke. From the point of contact, the configuration of the arms is maintained and accelerated so that the hands do not extend beyond the forearms, and maximum bat speed is maintained through impact. This is the same description of the process described by C.B. Fry for the swing of the cricket bat in general: half-arm-swing to the point of contact, and then full arm-swing through contact to initiate the follow-through.

Qualitative Optimisation Analysis: Front Foot Drive

Required Output: Front foot drive with power and control.

Cost Function: Time to execute stroke.

Design Variables:

1. Initial position - Modern Ranji Position
2. Bat downswing
3. Front foot movement
4. Back foot movement
5. Weight transfer

Constraints:

1. Head behind the ball with the eyes almost parallel

2. Initial hip and shoulders in line with direction of stroke

3. Vertical bat during stroke

The front foot drive according to the qualitative optimisation principles. This stroke is merely an extension of the front foot defensive stroke. If the biomechanics of the stroke is efficient, then the drive can be hit with tremendous power even if the back lift just extends above the waistline. This can give an important advantage against fast bowling, and during the beginning period of an innings when the margin for error is small.

This is the basic technique for all the drives with some variations. For the cover driven, contact is made later and usually behind the front leg. For the on drive, only a short step is repaired behind the line of the ball, and the ball hit in front of the instep. Also, the hips are allowed to turn early, so that he eyes can follow the stroke.

The on drive is played by taking only a small step on the leg side, and opening up the right hip. The ball is struck over the instep, and the foot must point towards the off side.

Try playing an on drive from the line of the of stump using the orthodox technique of pointing the front foot towards mid on! There are many times during the match when the batter must be able to break up the line of the bowler while at the same time minimising the risks. With the front foot pointing towards the off side it is possible to safely drive balls through the on side even when they pitch in line with off stump. Viv Richards and K. S. Ranjitsinjhi were great exponents of this method.

There is a traditional school of thought that does not believe in the lifting and turning of the rear foot as this is supposed to open up the hips, and therefore the shoulders, causing the batter to pull the bat across the line of the ball towards the leg side. However, if a correct closed hip alignment is maintained during the early stages of the lateral shift, and the weight transferred over a bent front knee with the foot pointing to the off side, this anatomically constrains the action of the hips, so that any excessive opening of the hips is prevented. Therefore, this argument cannot be sustained on biomechanical grounds. And of course, by keeping the rear foot solidly pegged to the ground throughout the entire stroke the weight cannot be optimally transferred into the stroke, the weight cannot be optimally transferred into the stroke, and it is more difficult to maintain a good head position behind the ball. This is another example of how a thoughtful qualitative optimisation analysis can easily dispel a troublesome technical myth that may surface from time to time. It is also a process that can be used by coaches who have some understanding of biomechanical principles often a detailed knowledge is not necessary. As long as the cost function, design variables and constraints are defined correctly, there is a good probability that an efficient technical solution will be found.

Note: *Some coaches suggest that the right foot turns well after ball contact in, and therefore does not play a part in transferring weight into the stroke. What they have failed to understand is that the turning of the right hip creates a 'follow-through' effect. It is not possible to instantaneously decelerate the body without undergoing some catastrophic process! For instance if a brick wall were placed at the end of a 100m track, then any sane sprinter would start to vigorously reduce speed before reaching the end of the race. Similarly, a pegged right leg inhibits the forward momentum of the body well before the time of ball contact. Also, this makes it more difficult to maintain a head position directly behind the ball, and make ball contact in front of the pad.*

Playing Spin Bowling

The techniques described previously apply equally against a spinning ball as it does for a fast one. However, there are some points we would like to make specifically on the art of playing spin bowling.

Of course, it is impossible to cover all the aspects on how to play spin bowling. Good spin bowlers have a large variety of deliveries, which are executed with a great deal of precision and subtlety. There is no prescribed recipe that can compact all types of spin bowlers. Each spin bowler is unique in technique, style, and personality. Each one releases the ball in a different manner even though the type of delivery may be the some. For example, though they are both wrist spinners there is little similarity in the methods of Chandrasekhar (India), who delivers leg-breaks, topspinners, and googlies at almost medium pace; and Warne (Australia), who delivers chiefly side-spinning leg breaks with a tilted back seam at a considerably slower pace. Also, consider Prasanna (India), who delivered off breaks with a sharp twist of the fingers, and made the ball drop sharply before reaching the batsman; and contrast this with Derek Underwood, who bowled left arm finger spin at around medium pace, and could decimate an entire batting side in quick time on a slightly dampish wicket.

Clearly, it can be argued that playing spin bowling is more an art than a science. However, there are still some important scientific principles that make the art of playing spin bowling far simpler. Consider the modern trend to play the ball behind the pad, often with the bat trailing well behind. This method of playing spin bowling is an admission of defeat! The batter has signified that the ball is too difficult to play with the bat. Apart from being a very negative method, it is also not a very successful one. Good spin bowlers continue to dominate betaine line ups throughout the world. Bowlers such as Muttiah Muralidharan, Saqlain Mustaq, Anil Kumble, and Shane Warne have often been the telling difference in a Test series. Even Australia, the most successful cricket team at the moment, has had tremendous difficulty in countering spin bowling on the subcontinent, losing convincingly against India and Sri Lanka recently. Even in Pakistan there was a time not long ago when they had not won a Test series in thirty eight years. England, New Zealand and the West Indies have also had their share of losses against quality spin bowling, particularly of the wrist spinning type. So what is responsible for this inability to play quality spin bowling when the pitch takes some turn? We suggest that is an inadequate technique that lies at the heart of the matter, particularly the method of playing with the bat behind pad.

Without going into full details, the optimal forward defensive stroke is best equipped to handle spin bowling. The bat is in front of the eyes, so the ball can be tracked more efficiently onto the bat. Shifting the hips forward and bending the knee transfers the weight forward. And, lifting the rear heel, and turning the rear foot to face the line of the intended stroke further facilitates this process. By playing forward in such a manner and moving the bat either inside (for an off spinner) or outside (for a leg-spinner) the line to compensate for the spin, the batter has the best chance to successfully counter the spinning ball with the bat. Note that this is different to playing forward to a ball and thrusting the bat well forward of the body. This is sometimes the perception when one talks about playing in front of the pad. This is much worse that playing behind the pad! The optimal forward defence has to employed to a ball that can be suitable smothered and the weight must be transferred well forward and down into the stroke.

There are advantages in playing in front of the pad. However to successfully use this technique, the batter must mentally 'look' to make contact with the ball in front of the eyes. If the bell should the unexpectedly change its trajectory or spin, the batter is in the best position to make the appropriate adjustment. In other words, playing in front of the pad does not mean play early. Instead, the batter must still wait for the ball, but with intention of making contact in front of the pad. This is the real art, but one that allows elite batters not only to negotiate sharply turning balls, but also work them away for runs. This is unlike the bat behind the pad position, which commits the batter to a defensive stroke at best.

Playing off spin off the front foot uses the same principles as for the standard defensive stroke. In this case, however, the author has taken his guard an leg stump and played slightly inside the line of the ball, so that the ball would turn onto the bat. Effectively, the is playing straight against the line of the oncoming ball, minimising the chances of a bat pad catch to any close in leg side fielders. Note that against spin bowling the rear leg straightens earlier than when playing medium or fast bowling because the weight must be transferred downwards into the ball at impact. To play leg spin off the front foot it is essential that the front foot point towards cover, because this makes it easier to move the leg outside the line of the ball. As the ball turns towards the off, the bat is brought over the instep, and contact made in front of the pad. The rear leg straightens early, and the rear foot lifted and turned so that the weight can be transferred downwards into the stroke.

Recently there has been much talk about the need for batters to jump or dance down the pitch to play spin bowling. Though running down the wicket is a basic cricket skill, without mastering the basic forward strokes little will be gained. It is impossible to jump down the wicket to a spinner every ball. If the batter has not mastered the basic front foot stroke, then he will be forced to move down the wicket at the inappropriate time. Also, certain bowers like Kumble, Chandraskhar, and Underwood do not give you the time to advance down the wicket during the ball's flight. To do so would give the bowler an advantage! Also, after advancing down the wicket, a forward stroke has to be played anyway, and the batter should still look to make contact in front of the pad. To play the ball behind the pad means the batter has to skip down that extra yard further. In addition, if the ball should be slightly misjudged in flight, which consistently happens against quality spinners, the batter is fully committed to the stroke with little chance of adjustment.

Another popular suggestion is to play the sweep shot extensively, even on the line of the stumps. There are coaching schemes in place where young players are taught that without playing the sweep shot they cannot be good players of spin bowling. The fact is that many of the great players of spin bowling, though they had it in their repertoire, did not use the sweep shot extensively Instead, they had very good command of the basic forward and back foot strokes.

We suggest therefore that the art of playing spin requires proficiency in the optimal methods of playing forward and back. Though advancing down the wicket and sweeping are useful strategies against spinners, the foundation should be built upon efficient front and back foot strokes. In particular, young batters should learn to play forward and defend a spinning ball with the bat rather than with the pad. Also they must learn to play back whenever the ball cannot be effectively smothered with the bat on the front foot. Pad play must be discouraged. In fact, often the key to dominating spinners lies in the batters's ability to play a forcing stroke off the back foot whenever the ball is fractionally short. By removing the need to be perfectly side-on for the back foot strokes, great power can be generated off the back foot when the lateral shift of the hips and arm wrist action are combined to hit the ball in front of the body. This would cause the spinner to change the length of delivery, and perhaps over-pitch, bringing the front foot drive into play. Contrary to common belief, it is the strong back foot player that poses the biggest threat to a spin bowler, particularly to those that mainly rely on obtaining their wickets through catches to close in fielders.

An example of what to do if an off spinner pitches slightly short of a length: move well back in a chest on position, and force the ball through the on side. Such strokes give the bowler less margin for error, and entice him/her to throw the ball further up to bat, increasing the probability of an over pitched delivery.

Finally, a word on the initial movement against spin bowlers. It has long been recognised that this should be a front foot movement as much of the play is off the front foot, and this also improves the ability to run down the wicket if required. However, it is also important for the initial movement not to compromise the ability to move back. A way of achieving this is to invert the Ranjitsinhji principle, and instead of moving back and across with the head forward, move forward slightly with the head kept in front, while placing slightly more weight on the back foot.

3

HORIZONTAL BAT STROKES

- Introduction
- The Cut Strokes
- The Pull and Hook Strokes
- The Sweep Shot

INTRODUCTION

When a ball is short, and does not threaten the batter in terms of dismissal or physical injury, then the horizontal bat strokes - namely the hook, pull and cut - may be used. Also, against spin bowling another horizontal bat stroke called the sweep can be used to good effect. In general, these have been adequately described by the current coaching literature, so they will not be treated extensively here. We will present only a basic summary of these strokes, and any elements that differ from the traditional approach.

The Cut Strokes

For balls pitched short of a good length and wide of the stumps, the cut-shot can be employed. The stroke begins by moving the back foot towards the off stump, and transferring the weight to the back leg. The back lift is higher than waist level, and is brought into the horizontal position with the left hand, at which point the wrists unwind and sharply hit down on top of the ball, the shot is most effectively played when the arms are close to full extension at ball contact. The open bat face in the Ranji position ensures that wrist action is optimised, and brings additional control to the stroke, providing that the stroke is initiated with the top hand. Power is automatically generated by the action of the hip and trunk segments. In the orthodox cut shot the front leg remains in contact with the ground. However, a modern version is top lift the front leg and bend it at the knee, allowing this segment to accelerate towards the midline of the body in response to the forces generated by the upper body. Both methods are sound; however, it is possible that the latter one gives more control against fast bowling, because the reaction of the bent front leg can osmeterium prevent the hips and shoulders from opening up too soon. The cut shot can be hit square or fine with equal facility. For the late cut shot, it is helpful to drop the bottom hand hear the splice of the bat. This gives additional control, and can make the late cut a powerful asset in a batter's repertoire.

***The Square Cut.* Move back and hit down on the ball with a horizontal blade, making sure that the arms are close to full extension at ball contact. Useful Tip: To give the sense of hitting down onto the ball, move back onto the ball of the rear foot.**

***The late cut* is played behind point, and extra control is achieved if the bottom hand slips down the handily. Also, the rear foot can point slightly behind point.**

The Pull and Hook Strokes

The pull stroke is usually played to a short pitched delivery or long hop that lands in line with or just outside the stumps. In response to such a delivery, the back foot must move back and across, with the emphasis on moving across to get outside the line of the ball. The bat is lifted high with the top hand, and the wrists cocked. The bat is brought down with the top hand in control by rotating the hips and trunk in the direction of the leg side. When the hands begin to travel in front of the body, the wrists undock and accelerate the bat to ball contact. The body continues to swivel until the rear shoulder faces the bowler. There are times when it is not possible to move outside the line of the ball, particularly when pulling a ball outside the off stump. Then a good rule of thump is to move across the necessary amount to make contact with the ball in front of the rear shoulder. The hook shot is played similarly, but used for balls that bounce over shoulder height. It is not advisable to hook any delivery unless the batter has sufficiently moved outside the line of the ball. Power for these strokes is supplied by the component segmental sequencing of the hips, trunk, and shoulders A modern version of the pull shot is not to move outside the line of the ball, but stay open-chested while accelerating a bent front knee towards the midline of the body; the theory is that the reaction caused by this movement will accelerate the shoulders. However, this puts the batter into an awkward and sometimes dangerous position. Power is actually diminished, because the movement of the front leg reduces the range of trunk rotation. This is different from the case when a batter lifts the front leg reduces the range of trunk rotation. This is different from the case when a batter lifts the front leg to give the feeling that the trunk is protected, particularly for deliveries that are travelling in line with the body. This is largely a psychological need than a mechanical one. The body still must complete a swivel with thew front leg in this bent position. It is possible that the bent front leg reduces the moment of inertia about the longitudinal axis of the body's centre of rotation, and thus facilitates the swivelling action. Bradman proposed one further advanced variation. He says

" Instead of putting the right foot back and across to the off side just put the fight foot straight back. Then, as the ball is hit between mid - on - and square leg, pull your body away from the line of flight as the left foot is swung round to the leg side whilst you pivot on the right foot. In this way tremendous power can be generated, even more than with the other method, because there seems to be scope for greater leverage. The whole mechanism of the wrists, arms and body can be harnesses to give the ball a tremendous crack. Should the ball be missed, it will pass on the off side of the body (and if it keeps low often with fatal results), because the ideal ball to pull in this way is one delivered on the stumps." **Bradman (1998)**

Bradman only used this pull shot under certain condition usually a straggliest ball on a wicket without too much pace which would enable him to hit the ball between mid-on and mid-wicket where there is often a significant gap. It must not be attempted when the ball is coming in towards the body, and must never be hit in the air, as this method can cause the ball to be mis-timed as the bat often meets the ball late, which would result in an easy catch in front of the wicket. To play this shot successfully the body must still swivel rapidly. However, this stroke should only be taught to advanced players, who have mastered the orthodox method. The danger is that young players may prefer the 'Bradman variation' and make gone straight back with the rear foot a habit that they take into other back foot strokes.

The correct way to pull- swivel about the rear foot to generate power and move the body inside the line of the ball. The key is to get into an open-chested position as early as possible by opening up the rear foot to face the bowler.

The Sweep Shot

The sweep shot can be played against a slow spinner, who consistently pitches the ball in line with leg stump. For off spinners it is possible to even sweep balls on the line of the stumps. It is more dangerous to sweep against leg-spin bowlers, particularly if they are consistently pitching the ball in the rough. However, if the leg-spinner is consistently bowling on a line outside leg stump, sometimes the seep must be employed. To play the sweep shot the bat must hit down onto the ball with a horizontal blade. The wrists must be cocked at the back lift, and the top hand initiate the downswing while the front leg bends and moves behind the line of the ball to form the second line of defence. The rear knee comes to rest on the ground. Then as the bat comes down to the meet the ball, the wrists are extended and hit down and across the line of the ball, hitting it behind square leg.

The Sweep Shot. **It is critical that the wrists are cocked at the top of the downswing and brought forward of the body, so that they can hit down onto the ball in a horizontal plane. The stroke is not really a sweeping type of motion, but a firm hit down onto the ball.**

The Glances

The glance strokes are simple extensions of the optimal defensive strokes on the leg-side. For the front foot leg-glance, a short step is taken with the front foot pointing to the off-side. The rear hip opens up quickly to the front, and contact is made with the ball in front of the pad by dropping the front elbow to the left and pushing the wrists forward. For the back foot leg-glance, a front-on position is obtained, and contact made in front of the body, as the wrists turn at impact.

To play the front foot leg glance, follow the principles of all front foot on side play: short step, front foot pointing towards the off-side, and rear hip turned towards the front. Before impact, start rolling the wrists, so that at impact the ball is angled behind square leg. A short backlift is required - the bat should be brought down early in front of the pad.

The back foot leg glance is executed when the chest is opened up to face the bowler. Contact is made in front of the body, and the wrists rolled onto the ball.

4

A BATTING SECRET—HOW TO AVOID EDGES

- **A Batting Secret How to Avoid Edges**
- **Some Erroneous Practices**
- **Final Remarks**

A Batting Secret How to Avoid Edges

The cricket bat cannot exceed 4.25 inches in width. To Counter a ball that may travel in excess of 90 miles per hour, and move side ways in the air or off the pitch with a varying degree of bounce, this thin piece of wood seems wholly inadequate. Therefore, it does not take much for a ball to deviate and take the edge of the bat. The biggest problem is for a batter, who has just arrived at the wicket against a swinging ball, when there are several slips and a gully in place. Indeed, nicking it to the slips seems almost inevitable. And, indeed, for the elite battery this is the most common form of early dismissal. Therefore, if the batter uses a method to reduce the likelihood of edging the ball to the slips, then the probability of making runs is significantly increased.

So, then what measures can be taken to safeguard against the ball that moves away? Sir Donald Bradman had this to say

" When in form I liked to feel in playing back defensively that I was hitting the ball towards the bawler of mid on rather than towards cover. It gave me a feeling of security that I was if anything, coming from outside the line of flight and therefore guarding against a possible slip catch from the ball which went away to the off. It is so much easier to follow the ball which goes towards the leg side." Bradman (1998)

In other works, to optimise the likelihood of making solid contact with the ball, present a full face to the ball by defending the ball as straight as possible towards the bowler. This way the full 4.25 inches is presented to the ball. Defensive shots towards cover probably present only half that much to the ball about 2.12 inches! When the figures are presented the argument becomes quite convincing. Bradman also talks about playing slightly outside the line of the ball. This means that if the ball does move away the bat is already partially in place to compensate for that movement. Of course, this technique is easier to use against fast bowlers, if the initial movement is back and across prior to delivery. Otherwise. There is less time to move outside the line of the ball. Also, ball contact must be made in front of the body, so that the bat is in a position to follow the ball to the leg side if there is less movement than anticipated, or indeed, if it moves in towards the body. It also goes without saying that a pure side-on back foot position with the foot oriented in the direction of point will inhibit the ability to adopt this strategy.

To guard against the outside edge, the batter should try whenever possible to move outside the line of the ball. Then if the ball should move away he is already covering for this movement. If there is no such away movement, or the movement is towards the leg side, the batter can play a glance type stroke through the leg side for perhaps one of two runs. Of course, this strategy will only work if the batter's feet are pointing in front of the batting crease, and contact is made well in front of the body.

On the front a foot a similar approach can be adopted. If the front foot strokes are executed with the font foot pointed towards extra-then it is easy to play straight down or slightly outside the line of the ball. Again, bat cognatic must occur in front of the body. Any movement away to the slips is then partially compensated for. However, any movement in towards the leg can also be countered by turning the wrists as in a glance. With the bat in front, and the eyes directly behind the ball, there is little that can go wrong. Finally, a word on how to miss the ball successfully! Even with the techniques described, it is not possible to hit every ball in cricket. There are balls that will move more than the amount that can be realistically compensated for. The art then is to play and miss, not play and nick! The great batters know how to play and miss the ball when the delivery has done too much. Generically, a sound method is to drop the wrists or play inside the ;line of the ball if it cannot be defended in are running from mid on to mid off. Bradman was a strong advocate of this principle. With his unique pronated grip, his blade was actually slightly closed at impact, so any deviations away to the slips more often than not passed harmlessly by the outside edge of the bat. It may look like the batter is continually playing and missing, and the bowler may think that he/she is very unlucky. However, the batter is scientifically missing the ball! Conversely, batters that continually 'nick' the ball to the wicket-keeper and slips are those that do not move into the correct position to defend the ball with the full blade of the bat. Instead, a majority of their defensive strokes are played towards cover or even point.

5

SOME ERRONEOUS PRACTICES

There have recently been some batting drills that were devised supposedly according to the principles of biomechanics. These drills are now becoming standard items of practice throughout the cricketing world. The purpose of this section is to briefly show why these drills run counter to principles of sound batting biomechanics.

The Inver drills

The Inver drill is performed with the objective of optimising driving power against a ball that is rolled along the ground towards the batter. To obtain maximum bat speed in this case, the batter uses a back lift above shoulder height, with the bat face open. The right elbow is pushed out and positioned under the bat. Then as the ball approaches, the bat is accelerated with the shoulders and pulled down with both arms. When the bat reaches about the level of the hips, the wrists start rolling as in a golf drive, and contact is made well behind the front foot with the body beside the ball. During the moment of contact, the wrists are accelerating bottom one over the top as in a golf swing, and the bat finishes across and over the leading shoulder during the follow through. Reasonable power can be generated in this stroke. However, it is difficult to see how this stroke is related to the drive in cricket. It has more similarities with the drive in golf. This is an example where biomechanics can go very wrong: when a qualitative optimisation approach is not performed within the appropriate constraints. Obviously the Inver drill is designed to optimise bat speed-but what are the constraints? The head and eyes are not behind the ball! This is a fundamental constraint in all vertical bat strokes. When this constraint is ignored, the stroke becomes irrelevant. In fact, the vertical bat constraint is violate as well. At contact, the left elbow is dropped, and the right shoulder brought around, rendering it almost impossible to maintain a vertical bat. Also, what about the cost function-i.e. Minimising the time to execute the stroke? A high back lift is required to generate power because ball contact is made behind the front leg, and the weight cannot therefore be wholly transferred into the ball.

The Inver Drill or the rolled ball drive. This drill does not develop driving skills within the constraints of the game. As such, it encourages the development of many technical faults in driving: head outside the line of the ball, front elbow dropping at contact, bat face rolling across the line of the ball at impact, weight not transferred fully, contact made behind the front leg, etc. In fact, the author is not an expert in the execution of this drill, and therefore not all the faults are exposed. For instance, in the classic version, the back lift is at shoulder height, and the right elbow moved well away from the right hip like Jack Nicklaus backswing in golf. Also the rear foot is not supposed to turn towards the front. All this leads the authors to conclude that this drill runs counter to most of the fundamental principles of efficient batting.

In fact, the drill itself does not conform to constraints of normal play. It is very rare that a ball rolls on the ground towards a batter in a match. Therefore, to design a drill with the purpose of optimising bat speed against this type of delivery is very difficult to justify rationally. It is indeed very surprising to see even experienced coaches using this drill to instruct young players on the are of driving. It is almost impossible to design another drill that goes so much against the basic fundamentals of technique in cricket. One may as well use the standard baseball stroke as a batting drill, and claim its usefulness based on the development of bat speed. The authors believe that the use of this drill poses the biggest threat to the development of young players, and strongly advise that it is removed from all coaching programers, particularly those that are designed for younger players.

***Notes*: Rolling the wrists can be used for front foot strokes through cover or finer; but these strokes are played differently from the vertical bat stragglier drives. The finer the stroke the more oblique the swing plane of the bat; this constrains the head to be inside the line of the ball as contact is made behind the front leg. In such cases, rolling the wrists adds to the power and control of the stroke. There may be other times when an experienced player will choose to play a drive by rolling the wrists, but this stoke is best left to the experts, and not a necessary one. For example, Sir Donald Bradman with his extreme pronated batting grip, i.e. the V of his top left hand runs to the bottom inside edge of his bat, could roll the wrists during the follow through of certain drives and yet maintain a vertical bat during the ball contact phase.**

Drop and Skip Drills

This drill involves two people-a batter and a dropper. The dropper is about 2-3 away from the batter, and drops a ball vertically from above the head. The batter then skips down the wicket using the cross over steep and strikes the ball on the half-volley with maximum bat speed. Unfortunately,

This well intentioned drill to aid a batter to run down the wicket against spin bowling does not conform to the correct technical constraints. Because the ball is dropped vertically and the batter has to hit the ball on the half volley while keeping it on the ground, it is not possible to strike the ball in front of the advancing leg. This is similar to the kind of stroke executed in the Inver-type drills: the weight is not transferred fully, a high back lift is used, the wrists roll over at impact, and the body and head are beside the line of the ball. Again, it is difficult to see how this drill is related to the art of playing spin bowling. To bat against spin bowling, the batter should mentally 'look' to make contact in front of the eyes. Quality spin bowlers continually change the trajectory of the ball's flight, so it is essential for the batter to adopt a position that allows for last minute adjustments to the stroke. This can only be achieved if the batter keeps the eyes behind the line of the ball with the intention of meeting the ball in front of the pad. To make contact with a ball under the eyes after skipping down the wicket would require the batter to travel further and quicker, as well as decide very early on in the ball's flight the landing position of the ball. There is little chance of effective stroke adjustment should the need arise. Also, it is totally impractical to roll of the wrists at impact against a spinning ball, which usually possesses a hefty component of topspin. There would be a good chance of lifting the ball. Again, the design of this drill is an example of a pseudo-biomechanical effort to optimise bat speed without considering the appropriate technical Constraints.

The drop and skip drill was designed to improve a batter's ability to run down the wicket to counter spin bowling. Unfortunately, it encourages the development of the same technical errors as in the Inver drill. It is difficult to understand how a spinning ball can be consistently played with the intention of striking it behind the front leg while the eyes are not behind the line of the ball. Also the bat face is being rotated sharply upon impact with the bottom hand. Clearly, any ball that is not judged precisely will result in a lofted stroke. It is difficult to demonstrate this drill, because the principles underlying it run counter to those of efficient batting.

Final Remarks

The purpose of batting is to score as many runs as possible within a reasonable period of time. To do this, the batter has to occupy the crease. Many of the principles we have discussed serve a dual purpose: to increase options, and to decrease the probability of dismissal not just to increase bat speed! Therefore, the methods we have proposed are designed to increase the run-scoring ability of batters.

Technically, we have formulated a new conceptual framework in which to optimise batting performance. Concepts such as bat position, lateral hip shift, lifting the rear foot, the Ranjitsinjhi principle, and the C.B. Fry Swing theory are a radical departure from the traditional description of batting technique. However, they have been conceptualised according to a qualitative optimisation method, and evidence of their effectiveness is found in the techniques of the world's most elite batters.

A look at the batting statistics of the world will show a huge gap between the world's greatest batsman ever, Sir Donald Bradman, and the rest. An average of 99.94 is staggering, but it is still surprising that no-one else has even averaged in the 70's, in any era of cricket. The great batsmen are considered to average over 50, and the good ones over 40. However, this is still such a long way from 'the Don'. It is true. Perhaps, that in the modern game it is not possible to score like Bradman, because the game has changed significantly-bowlers are faster and fitter, fielding standards are much higher, and so on. But, why were there not any other batsmen in Bradman's era that averaged in the 60's let alone the 90's Even though bowling and fielding standards have become more professional, there is still the argument that perhaps the techniques of the elite batsmen in the world, are not optimal, and therefore batting averages are lower than they should be. Alternatively, it can be argued that secret of Bradman's success lay in his wonderful eyesight and reflexes Or, that he had a phenomenal strength of mind Whatever the case, the purpose of this article is to show how a qualitative biomechanical analysis of batting technique can provide coaches with the means to improve batting performance when the appropriate constraints are defined. No doubt these techniques can be further refined, and the qualitative analysis method improved, but we believe that the essential techniques described here have the potential to significantly improve a batter's making ability. And, perhaps, it is possible for elite batters like Sachin Tendulkar, Bran Lara and Steve Waugh to average in the 70s rather than the 50s.

We also believe that the techniques developed in this article should be incorporated into the national training programs of cricket playing countries. This would particularly benefit those countries that do not have either the population or resources to compete with the top playing nations of the world. It is important in this case to increase the number of quality players by teaching them the cricket skills that really do improve performance.

6

ANALYSIS OF SIMPLE BOWLING

Introduction

There is little doubt that the great diversity of styles and techniques of bowlers from countries enjoying test match status has helped to shape the history of cricket. With the recent world-wide implementation of professional coaching schemes, which generally teach only one, or perhaps two optimal ways of delivering a ball, bowling could be in danger of losing its technical diversity. Are we therefore on the verge of a new era in which the art of bowling is irretrievably lost? Possibly! However, as discussed below, the biomechanical principles underlying the bowling technique reveal some interesting new facts.

For those less well acquainted with the game of cricket, the technique of bowling must seem exceedingly simple. Just use a straight arm to release a ball at a suitable speed to cover a distance of 22 yards bouncing only once off the ground before reaching the batter. If so simple, how could the execution of such an action in a cricket match hold the attention of millions of people for 3,4 or 5 days at a stretch? And why would particular individuals, called bowlers, spend countless hours perfecting their art in the practice nets, only to spend countless more hours on the cricket field, often under the most trying of conditions, to deliver balls at a stationary batsman?

Those who know the game intimately are aware of the reasons for such rigorous practice. Bowling is an art of infinite subtlety, not only in strategy, but also in its most basic mechanics. The bowler has an almost unlimited array of variations to help confound the batsman-from varying the pace, the length (the distance travelled before bouncing), and the line of delivery to swinging and swerving: motions dependent on the intricate combination of the seam angle and spin are also used to change the line of the ball off the pitch.

It is evident then that the physics of bowling is immensely complex, and not fully understood. In this article, only one aspect of bowling is discussed, the one that is probably the most important: the biomechanics of bowling. Some coaches believe that the mechanics of bowling is relatively simple, and that the basic side-on action is the option is the optimal technique. However, a proper understanding of the biomechanical principles underlying bowling reveals that this is in no way the case.

The Basic Bowling Technique

For those not familiar with cricket, a brief account of the basic bowling technique (right-hand bowler) will serve as a useful introduction.

After a run-up to generate momentum, the bowler leaps into the air with the back arched, and the head behind a high left arm, which is bent towards the right shoulder. The bowling arm (right arm) at this stage is bent and close to the body with the hand about face level, and the trunk leaning backwards and laterally. Then as the right foot contacts the ground, the straightening of the left arm is synchronised with that of the bowling arm as it drops towards the level of the hips. Once the bowling arm is fully straightened ("locked"), the left arm is pulled downward facilitating the circular swing of the bowling arm about the shoulder joint as the shoulder joint as the trunk begins to flex forwards. This process continues until the ball is released off the left foot, and the "follow-though" is initiated when the bent right leg steps past the front leg.

Models of Bowling

It appears that much of the cricket literature on bowling technique is generated purely from the experience of past players. Though there has been some excellent research into the biomechanics of injuries sustained by fast bowlers, most other attempts to understand the biomechanics of bowling have been limited to the analysis of kinematic and force plate data. This has played a part in the development of the bowling technique, but is inadequate to understand the underlying mechanics of bowling. The University of Walkout (*Dept. of physics & Electronic Engineering, and Dept. of Mathematics).* Hematin, is now generating the first mathematical models of bowling in an attempt to understand bowling techniques and thus improve coaching methods. A physical action, such as bowling a ball, is often difficult to understand if considered throughout in all its complexity. On the human body can be represented as a system of interconnected rigid body segments subject to applied external forces and torques. A segment could be, for example, a forearm, a thigh or any other major body part attached by a hinge to other.

There are two general approaches of rigid body modelling within the field of classical dynamics: the direct method of analysis by applying Newton's laws to each of the individual parts of the system: or a more indirect method, which treats the system as a whole by using a comprehensive theory of mechanics based on energy principles. This latter method is known as Lagrangian mechanics, and can often be used to formulate a complete set of ordinary differential equations for the motion without solving explicitly for the constraint forces acting on the various parts of the system. It is caravanserais by its simplicity and is applicable in any suitable coordinates.

Once the Lagrangian equalitarians for a particular bowling model have been generated, it becomes possible to investigate the dynamics for a variety of bowling actions. This process reveals several interesting features of the bowling technique. In fact many of these are at odds with what is traditionally thought to constitute proper bowling technique. It is time, therefore, to allow biomechanics to dispel many of the myths that surround the bowling technique. However, this article is not intended to be the definitive account of bowling biomechanics. Research into bowling is still in its infancy and there is a long path to follow before many of its mysteries are revealed. What is presented here will help clear up some fundamental misunderstandings on the subject, and shed some light on the diverse and intricate field of bowling biomechanics.

7

MECHANICAL ANALYSIS OF CRICKET BOWLING

Recently I came across something on cricket bowling in my old departmental files that may be of interest to anyone who lives in the cricket playing countries of the world. The following preliminary biomechanical analysis carried out by one of our graduate students in the School of Mechanical Engineering at the University of the Witwatersrand on the controversial bowling action of one of south Africa's remarkable spin bowlers, Paul Adams.

This student has now moved to the University of Cape Town, where he is fortunate to be under the excellent supervision of Dr Kit Vaughan who returned to S Africa after teaching for many years in North America. Apparently he has now extended this work considerably and will be taking this project even further when he completes his Masters in the near future. As a cricked fan of many years standing and a keep university level player for several years, I look most forward to seeing what emerges from this research. It would be interesting to hear from others of any more up-to date work that must have been done on the mechanics of both spin and quick bowling. What is of special interest to me are the kinesiological differences between the delivery actions of cricket bowling and baseball pitching, especially since the ballistic winding up action in baseball seems to produce a large number of rotator cuff injuries. Even if one examines the throwing actions of top crocheting fielders and baseball fieldsmen (not necessarily bowlers or pitchers), the baseballer appears to use a far greater degree of lateral rotation of the humerus. Has anyone here come across a comparison of the normal throwing actions of cricketers and baseballers to ascertain which technique is more efficient and safer? Certainly, the situation and types of delivery are different to suit the game, but it would still be interesting to have a few more facts and figures about delivery styles as they relate to release velocity, ball control, shoulder integrity and so forth. Any offers?

8

ANALYSIS OF CRICKET BOWLING ACTION OF PAUL ADAMS

A recent video analysis of the unusual bowling action of south African spin bowler, Paul Adams, carried out during early 1996 in the School of Mechanical Engineering at the University of the Witwatersrand by postgraduate student, Dudley Tabakin, under the supervision of senior lecturer, Dr Mel Siff, revealed that a degree of elbow straightening may well be one of the secrets which allows Paul to impart remarkable spin to the ball. This preliminary study constituted the first scientific analysis or the controversial Adams action and should help the cricketing fathers replace current speculation with some hard evidence. During the previous year, Siff, in examining the differences baseball pitching and cricket bowling, had noticed what appeared to be a definite type of throwing action by Adams, that differed significantly from that of other international spinners with apparent 'chucking' actions, so, when Tabakin approached him about pursuing a Masters degree in biomechanics, Dr Siff suggested that he carry out a scientific analysis of the differences between the delivery actions in cricket and baseball. Tabakin began by analysing available video footage of Paul's bowling recorded during the recent matches between South Africa and England in South Africa, as well as on recordings of over that Paul bowled against the West Indies. Joint markers were identified on the neck, shoulder, elbow and wrist and these were digitised for every sequence of frames. He then analysed the data on a computer to determine the different joint angles for each bowling delivery. Some of the resulting graphs had to be discarded because they were either difficult to interpret or inaccurate. The example below offered one of the colorist and most accurate analyses of this video material. Point A marks the end of the preparatory and final winding up stage which characterises Paul's unique action. Here the elbow is thrust strongly backwards until it reaches its minimum value of 22 degrees. Since the triceps muscle crosses the elbow and shoulder joints, this action prostrates the triceps muscle and appears to allow Paul to subsequently use the stored elastic energy in this muscle to deliver a sharp thrust during the final straightening of his elbow. His arm continues to move backwards and upwards from position A until it reaches a point B diagonally behind his head where the major twisting action of his arm begins. His elbow angle at this point is 151 degrees. The twisting of all the joints of his arm (upper extremity) continues until the ball is released at point C, when his elbow angle has increased to 170 degrees. In other words, between points B and C, he has straightened his elbow by 19 degrees. According to the laws of cricket, the bowler may not change the angle of the elbow during the final delivery stage, so that this video analysis would imply that this action should be deemed to be throwing. Dr Siff considers that, because the anti-choking law was originally instituted to prevent fast bowlers from gaining an unfair speed advantage by bending and straightening the elbow, far less attention was paid to the spinning advantage offered to spin glowers by this type of elbow action. Since elbow action. Since elbow flexion allows the forearm to impart far greater spin to the ball (and better disguise of the action), even if the elbow is not straightened during delivery, while comparable slight elbow straightening by a fast bowler offers only a small increase in speed, it appears that a bent elbow offers a much greater advantage to a spinner than a fast bowler. This preliminary analysis suggests either that umpires adopt a stricter view towards spinners or that the laws of cricket be modified to allow some elbow straightening by all bowlers (provided that the elbow is not allowed to provide a sideways chucking action). Dudley is currently analysing many types of throwing and bowling actions as part of his Master's degree to offer scientific guidelines to the cricketing community concerning this problem. By the time that he has studied sufficient footage of Adams and other local and international sinners and quick bowlers, it is hoped that the cricketing world will be enriched by a better understanding of the different types of bowling action. Possibly this sort of analysis will even assist the cricketing fraternity in modifying and applying the laws of game. The aphorism, "It's not cricket", may then take on a entirely new meaning!

9

THE MECHANICS OF BOWLING

The high speed motion analysis systems at the University of Auckland (Dept. of Sport & Exercise Science) and the Waikato Polytechnic (Dept. of Sport & Exercise Science, Hamilton) were used to obtain kinematic data of various bowlers. By substituting this data into the Lagrangian equations of motion governing a particular bowling model, the joint torques could be calculated over time, thus giving a unique perspective into the dynamics of the bowling action.

Basic Action Type: There are two basic types of bowling action in cricket; the side on action and the front on action. The side on bowler looks behind the front arm during delivery stride to sight the target, while the front on bowler looks inside the front arm to achieve this end, causing the hips and shoulders to open and more or less face the batsman before delivery.

The side on action has generally been considered the orthodox method of bowling, most likely to achieve the best results. This paradigm was further perpetuated by early research, which suggested that the front on action was more likely to put strain on the lower lumber region, and therefore increase the risk of serious back injury. These findings were not in keeping with common experience, as at the time some of type world's most successful fast bowlers were from the West Indies, using predominantly front on actions with a relatively low incidence of reported back injury. Fortunately, common sense did eventually prevail, and more recent research has vindicated the front on action. Ironically, it may even be the safest action of them all!

However, there are still certain coaches who are suspicious of the front on action. Often reasons such as reduced accuracy and lack of away movement are cited. Yet, there have been many great exponents of this form of bowling. Malcolm Marshall, Curtly Amborose, Bod Willis, and Mike Procter-just to name a few have proved that front on bowlers can generate express pace and then the magical wizard from Pakistan, Abdul Qadir, really confounded the critics, when he conclusively proved that leg breaks could be bawled most destructively from a front on action Later, Mushtaq Ahmed, also from Pakistan, showed that even front-on leg-break bowlers with considerable less ability than Qadir, can still win Test Matches!

Run Up: Determining the purpose of a bowler's run up is relatively simple, but it is still subject to much confusion. There is a common belief that the main purpose of generating run up speed is to make a simple additive contribution to ball speed at release. It is likened to the case where a person throws an object forwards out of a moving train. The faster the speed of the train, the faster the object is released relative to the earth.

Is there any evidence to suggest that the additive principle of run-up speed is indeed utilised by bowlers to a significant extent? Previous studies have indicated that the run-up speed of very fast bowlers during the pentlandite stride is rarely above 20 km/h. In fact, Jeff Thomson probably the fastest bowler in the history of cricket only clocked up a run-up speed of 13.7 km/h during his penultimate stride. Considering that Thomson bowled his fastest balls at around 158 km/h, the additive contribution of his run-up is minimal.

Is the run-up therefore of minor importance to bowling? Or is there another principle at work?

Simple Lagrangian models and studies of force plate date from javelin throwers indicate that the run-up generates ball speed by utilising the ground reaction forces to initially slow the lower body, and then use the front leg as a lever. When a bowler is forced to decelerate during delivery stride, the inertia of the upper body helps trust the trunk and bowling arm forward over a braced front leg. So then why hasn't this reasoning been applied to the run-up? I am not sure, but it, really does seem that the purpose of having a run-up is for the very reason that one has to stop! All good javelin throwers use this principle. Coaches should change their emphasis on how them analyses and perhaps design the ideal run-up of a bowler. They should design the length, speed and rhythm of a run-up so that the bowler can brake quickly using the ground reaction forces to create a solid base of support over which the upper body segments can catapult themselves forward. Only then can the momentum generated by the run-up be transferred to the ball.

It must also be recognised that a run up must be individually tailored to suit the individual bowler, and accommodate technical differences. For instance, previous studies have indicated that run-up approach speeds of front-on bowlers are significantly faster than their side-on counterparts.

It may be destructive for a javelin-type bowler like Thomson to significantly increase his run-up speed based on the fact that Malcolm Marshall (a front-on bowler) runs in about twice at fast. Because a proper utilisation of the run up is concerned primarily with optimising the braking power, what suits one bowler is unlikely to suit someone using a different action.

Trunk Flexion: Another critical feature in bowling technique, which is not properly understood, is the role of trunk flexion in the generation of ball release see. It is commonly held that there is correlation between trunk flexion speed and ball release speed. Some coaches believe that the range of trunk extension-flexion angle is also important. Though these can be important factors, the reality of the trunk action in bowling is more complex.

During the delivery leap there is an initial trunk rotation and extension away from the intended direction of the ball. Once in delivery stride, the trunk begins to rotate and flex forwards pulling the bowling arm with it. However, there is a braking action on the trunk as it nears the end of its range of motion. By means of Newton's Third Law the braking action of the trunk segment further accelerates the bowling arm segments prior to shall release. Therefore, part of the reason why the trunk undergoes flexion is sop that it can decelerate at the appropriate time during delivery stride. The braking action of the trunk is perhaps one reason why fast bowlers of similar speed can deliver the ball with significantly different trunk extension angles and trunk flexion rates.

Action type also plays a major part in determining the amount of trunk flexion used to generate speed. Jeff Thomson, for instance, used to bowl with an exaggerated backward lean. Malcolm Marshall, on the other hand, bowled from a more vertical trunk position. In general, front-on bowlers do not extend the trunk as far as their side on counterparts. They may not need to as they can probably utilise their run-ups more efficiently.

Non-bowling Arm: Conventionally, it is taught that the non-bowling arm should be held high during the delivery leap and then, from the time of back foot contact, be pulled down vigorously to aid in the generation of ball speed. However, this is only an approximation to what is really the case.

Contribution to the action of the trunk is the motion of the non-bowling arm, but the mechanics of front-arm motion is complex, and a simple mechanical treatment can only alleviate some of the confusion surrounding it. By simulating simple rigid body models of the trunk and non-bowling arm produced an arm, it was shown that a clockwise torque exerted on the non-bowling arm produced an anti-clockwise reactive torque on the trunk. This is contrary to what is generally taught: that a clockwise pulling down motion of the non-bowling arm increases the rate of trunk flexion. Though it is anatomically necessary for the non-bowling arm to be pulled down somewhat, there should be more emphasis on its being pulled in towards the trunk, so that anti-clockwise torques are placed on the non-bowling arm.

Still there are other aspects of non-bowling arm action, which have to be considered. For instance, in certain actions it appears that there are phases in which the bowling arm does not rotate independently of the trunk. There may be phases in the bowling action when the bowling arm and trunk move as "one-piece". When this occurs it is more appropriate to say that trunk flexion is aided because the centre of gravity of the upper body as a whole is shifted forward, rather than by any action of front arm torques.

Also, the non-bowling arm should only be pulled in when the trunk is flexing. When the trunk undeterred its braking motion, it is vitally important that the action of the non-bowling arm is stopped. This is rarely taught properly, because bowlers are often cloned to tuck the non-bowling arm into the ribs during this time to forcible retard its motion. However, there is plenty of pictorial evidence to suggest that great bowlers, past and present, use a variety of methods to retard the non-bowling arm. Shane Warne blocks his front arm on the front leg during delivery stride. Contrast this with Dennis Lillee who seems to retard the front arm beside the left side of his body

Rear Hip: The correct action of the rear ship is one of the most important aspects of bowling. However, what is "correct" in this case is very difficult to determine. There is variation among successful bowlers. But in general, by accelerating the hip forward with a flexed knee, the bowler is likely to feel two effects: (1) a reactive force pulling the trunk towards it, and (2) a deceleration in the rotation of the bowling arm. So, for instance, if during a phase of the bowling action, the bowling arm is accelerating relative to the trunk, then the hip action should be retarded, as this would tend to decelerate the bowling arm.

This may reflect the situation for many finger-spinners, who can use more arm in their actions than other forms of bowling. The common teaching, therefore, to thrust the rear hip forward early with the knee bent once front foot contact without any consideration for the type of bowler, is technically erroneous and potentially damaging to bowling performance. Correct hip action is a subtle art requiring exquisite timing, and the mechanics behind it is still not well understood.

Front Knee Action: Coaches are often found admonishing young bowlers with the famous catch phrase " bowl over a braced front leg". This is an unfortunate situation, as the action of the front knee during delivery stride is complicated to understand mechanically. In fact, it is extremely difficult to determine the optimum knee action in bowling, and most likely, correct knee action is going to vary with the type of bowler and style of delivery.

Theoretically, apart from perhaps giving the bowler a slight leverage and height advantage, breeching the front leg causes a slight deceleration in trunk flexion. This means that if a bowler is to adopt a "braced front leg" technique, it must be executed during the phase of trunk decelerating for maximum efficiency. This is difficult to do if it is not natural, and that is why so many successful bowlers do bowl over a bent front knee-Wasim Akram, Andy Roberts, Bill O'Reilly, and Dennis Lillee-just to name a few! However, this is not to say that bracing the front leg should be discouraged. Only that coaches have to be aware that there is no one optimal knee action for all bowlers, and that careful consideration must be given before any changes are made here.

The Reality of Bowling: Technical diversity

It is evident from what has been discussed in this article so far, that bowling is a complex activity, which lends itself to a diverse range of techniques. This is because the act of bowling is said to be redundant, i.e. an infinite set of joint positions can lead the end effector (in this case the hand) to the same location. This same property can be demonstrated if you sit at a table and place a glass in front of you so that it can be easily pocked up with a bent arm. Notice how there are a variety of joint configurations that would allow you to carry out this task. This is somewhat the same case for the bowler trying to deliver a ball. There are many modes of delivery available.

So how many different types of allowable actions are there? An infinite number? Perhaps not, but lets run a simple example using an elementary combinatorial method to see if we can get a qualitative feel for the technical diversity in bowling. Let's assume that there are three allowable hip and shoulder alignments-closed, partially open (450), and open; two allowable front knee angles at ball release-straight (or braced) and bent: two different front-arm positions at back foot concatenate and straight; two heights of the front knee at back foot contact high and low; two positions at which the bowling arm straightens (or locks) early and late; there different orientations of the front hand at back foot contact towards the off-side towards the batsman, and towards the umpire; two different lifting actions of the rear leg during delivery late and early; three lengths of delivery stride-short, medium and long; three varieties of bowling arm action- rotary windmill type (hand has circumscribed two revolutions by release), standard type (hand starts in front of face or shoulder), and javelin-type (hand starts behind right hip). Considering only these variations, how many allowable actions are there? The answer is $3 \times 2 \times 2 \times 2 \times 2 \times 3 \times 2 \times 3 \times 3$, with gives a staggering 2592!

Imagine that! There are so many distinct ways of delivering a cricket ball, even when only the most basic of variations are considered. Of course, there are likely to be inter relationships between some of the technical variations. For instance, javelin-type actions are most likely to be used with closed hip and shoulder alignments. Such interrelationships will reduce the number of allowable actions. However, only the most basic variations have been considered here. For instance, the technical variations associated with spin and swing have not been considered. In reality, the number of allowable actions will be significantly higher, especially when the effects of individual differences in anthropometry are taken into account.

It may be argued that these variations are meanly stylistic in nature and have little to do with the biomechanical efficiency of the bowling action. For some variations observed in bowlers, this may be the case; but certainly not for the fundamental variations just considered here. Also, when the bowling action is modelled mathematically, it has been found that many of the movements in bowling which are often dismissed as merely stylistic embeliishments have actually been found to play a critical biomechanical role in the delivery of the ball.

10

CONCLUSION

Bowling is an art that cannot be reduced to a rigid set of mechanical principles. Ironically, it is only a proper application of biomechanics to bowling which reveals this. There is likely to be opposition to this point of view, because by nature people are uncomfortable when things cannot be concretely conceptualised. Einstein once said, “ Make things as simple as possible, but no simpler !” coaches often confuse “simple” with “simplistic” in their bid to reduce the art of bowling to understandable proportions. This is like trying to completely understand the art of classical music composition by developing a set of simple mathematical formulae for melody.

Yet others may be angered by the thought that the author proposes some sort of bowling anarchy, where anything goes. They would claim that coaching bowlers could become impossible-bowling is just to complex; non-one knows thousands of actions! And even if they did, who is to know which one suits whom. And this is my point exactly! The coaching of bowlers is an art too! There are often no easy answers! It requires the coach to have an in depth knowledge of the art of bowling, and this is somewhat dependent on the coach's playing experience and level of intuition. Without these, a coach could do more harm than good!

Bowling is a dynamic, flexible and creative art, where the participant takes part in a sort of rhythmic dance. In the past, there have been attempts to use science to reduce bowling to a set of recipe-like instructions. Perhaps this is what is causing many young bowlers to suffer serious back injuries? However, in the future, if biomechanics is utilised correctly to explain technical diversity rather than to shun it, then the art of bowling will be rediscovered, and displayed in all its wonder throughout the cricketing world and beyond.